The Story of a Special Day
Volume 114

April
23

The 113th day of the year (114th in leap years. There are 252 days remaining until the end of the year.

by Michael Dobson

Timespinner
Press

This book is also available in e-book form for Kindle, e-pub devices, and other formats from your favorite online booksellers.

For more information about the series, about us, or about your special day, please email us at editor@timespinnerpress.com.

Look for other volumes in *The Story of a Special Day,* coming often. See www.timespinnerpress.com for details and for the most recent information.

Table of Contents

Cover: A stained glass window portraying St. George and the dragon (Credit: G. Freihalter, CC BY-SA 3.0). The window itself is in the tomb of G. Bimar at the Père Lachaise Cemetery in Paris. St. George died on April 23, 303 — the EVENT OF THE DAY.

Quote of the Day

"Lord, what fools these mortals be!"

William Shakespeare, poet and playwright
in *A Midsummer Night's Dream*
Shakespeare died April 23, 1616

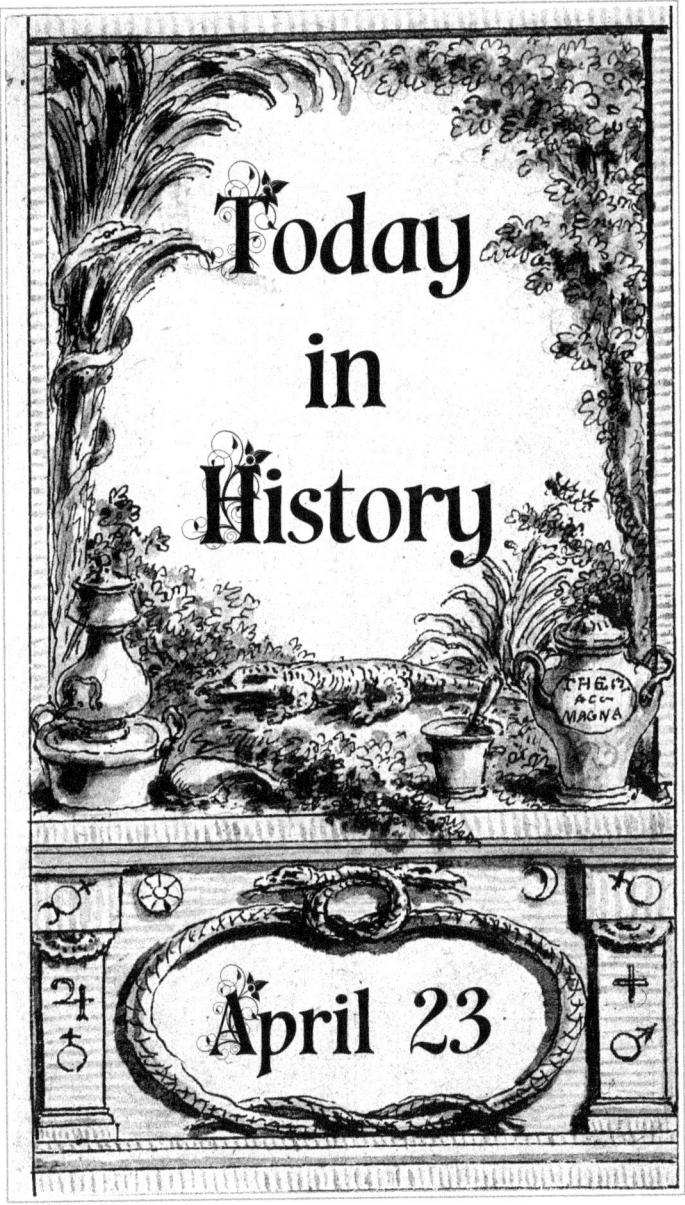

Today in History

April 23

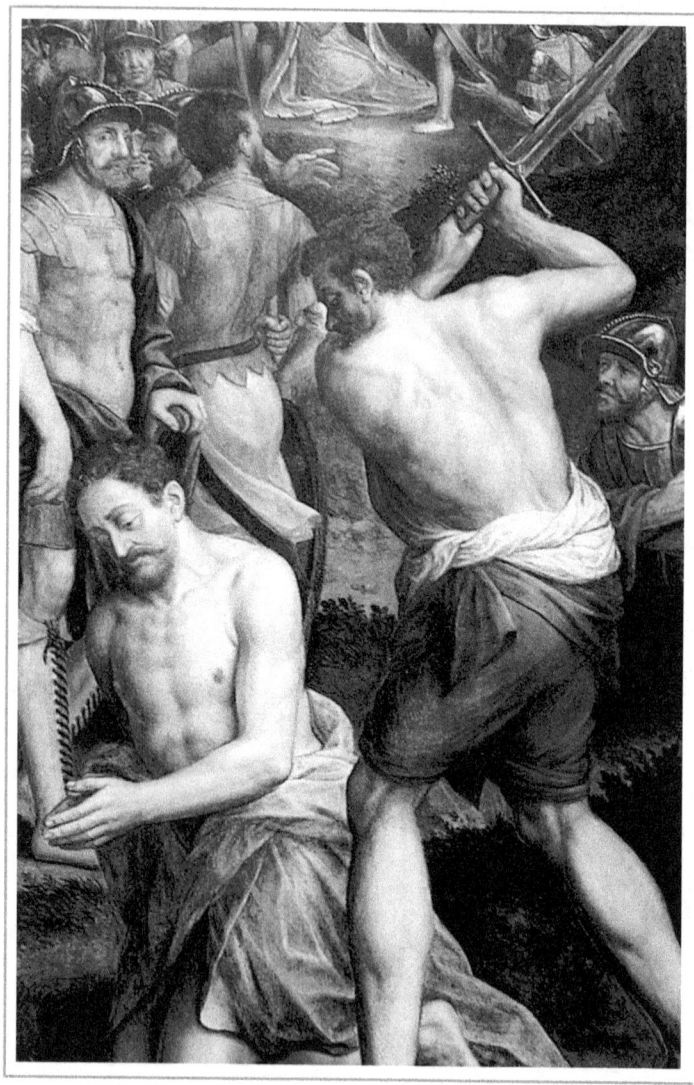

"The Torture of St. George," Michiel Coxie (circa 1580)

Event of the Day
The Martyrdom of St. George

In February of the year 303 CE*, the Roman Emperor Diocletian issued an edict that every Christian soldier in his army be arrested, and that every other soldier should make a sacrifice to the Roman gods. One of the tribunes in his Imperial Guard, George, approached the emperor to argue, but when Diocletian did not relent, George publicly proclaimed in front of his fellow soldiers that he was indeed a Christian.

Reluctant to condemn one of his best soldiers, Diocletian made several attempts to convert George back to the Roman religion. He offered George gifts of land, money, and slaves if he would only make a single sacrifice to the gods of Rome, but George continued to refuse.

When George continued to refuse, Diocletian sentenced him to torture, but meanwhile George had given all his wealth to the poor and prepared himself for martyrdom. He was lacerated on a wheel of swords three times, and when he still would not relent, Diocletian had him executed by decapitation on April 23, 303.

---

* For an explanation of "CE," see "On Names and Dates."

His suffering caused Diocletian's wife, the Empress Alexandra, as well as Athanasius, a pagan priest, to convert to Christianity, and they were executed along with George. Both George and Alexandra were later canonized as saints.

The Diocletianic Persecution

As with many people in ancient times, it's impossible to say with certainty that Saint George was a historical figure, or that the story surrounding his martyrdom is fact. However, the persecution of Roman soldiers by Diocletian is well documented. It was the last, and by far the most severe, persecution of Christians in the Roman Empire, and it was significantly aimed at the professional military class.

The earliest known text mentioning Saint George dates from the 5th century. From that and other early sources, Saint George was born to a Greek Christian family in Syria; his father, Gerontius, was also a Roman officer. Before his martyrdom, he had served faithfully for many years.

Saint George and the Dragon

For many people, the best known part of the story of Saint George is the one that is almost certainly mythological, the story of Saint George and the Dragon. This story originated in the East, and was brought to Europe by crusaders in the 11th century.

"Saint George Killing the Dragon," by Albrect Dürer

The story is set in a small town called Silene, in what is today Libya. A plague-bearing dragon had made its home in a small lake nearby, and was poisoning the countryside. To keep the dragon from rampaging, the villagers fet the dragon two sheep each day, and once they ran out of sheep, they began feeding their children to the dragon, with a lottery determining which would be sacrificed.

When the lottery chose the king's daughter as the next sacrifice, the king offered all his gold and silver and half his kingdom in place of his daughter, but the people refused. Dressed as a bride, the daughter was sent out to the lake to be sacrificed to the dragon.

By chance, Saint George rode past the lake and saw the princess. She tried to send him away before the dragon could eat him, but Saint George refused. When the dragon emerged from the lake, George made the sign of the Cross and charged the dragon on horseback, wounding it with his lance. He tied a leash around the wounded dragon and led it back to Silene, where he offered to kill the dragon if the inhabitants would convert to Christianity. Some fifteen thousand people, including the king, agreed, and Saint George slew the dragon.

Veneration of Saint George

In part because of the dragon myth, Saint George was widely venerated in the East. A basilica devoted to the saint in the town of Lydda in what is now Israel was burnt twice during the Crusades.

It was rebuilt each time; the current church, built in 1872, is still standing.

As a warrior saint, George was popular with military men. Although the dragon legend had not yet reach Europe, Saint George was venerated in England (which later declared him their national saint, as did Russia, Malta, Romania, and other countries) as early as the 8th century, and by the Middle Ages, many European nations had devotions and shrines dedicated to him. Saint George was called upon by Christians to aid them in battle, and visions of Saint George were reported in several battles.

The Union Jack, flag of the United Kingdom, consists of the Cross of Saint George (red cross on white background), representing England; the Cross of St. Andrew (white "X" on a blue background) for Scotland, and the Cross of St. Patrick (red "X" on white background) for Northern Ireland.
(Photo: Vaughn Leiberum, CC BY-SA 2.0)

In the East, where Saint George was originally best known, he is called "The Great Martyr." Images and icons of Saint George are common.

Interestingly, Saint George is also known and revered among Muslims in Asia Minor and the Levant, where he is known as al-Khadir (الخضر), a servant of God who has great wisdom and mystical knowledge. The stories of al-Khadir, however, are quite different from those of Saint George. He has also been associated with the Prophet Elijah and even Moses. Zororastrianism acknowledges the "green saint" (the Arabic word for green being *khadra*).

Saint George's Day is celebrated in numerous places, though on different dates. In Newfoundland and Labrador, it's the Monday closest to April 23. In many Eastern Orthodox nations, Saint George's Day is held on May 6 in the Gregorian calendar because that day corresponds to April 23 in the Julian calendar.[†]

Regardless of calendar type or nation, Saint George is one of the most beloved and honored saints worldwide.

[†] For an explanation of Gregorian and Julian calendars, see "What Day of the Week is April 23?"

"The Fair of Saint George's Day," by Peter Brueghel the Elder
(Courtesy Google Art Project)

A tray of beer served at the Brauereigasthof Rothenbach in Aufseß,
Bavaria, Germany (Photo: Ben Reis, CC BY-SA 3.0)

What Happened on April 23?

From the creation of great works of engineering and art, to devastating wars and natural disasters, thousands of years of history have left their mark on each and every day of the year. Here are some important events that occurred on April 23. (Illustrated items are boxed.)

1348 — The **Order of the Garter**, the highest order of chivalry in the United Kingdom, is founded by Edward III.

1516 — The **German Beer Purity Law** *(Reinheitsgebot)* is adopted in Bavaria.

1635 — The **oldest public school in the United States,** the Boston Latin School, opens. It remains one of the top 20 high schools in the US.

1914 — Construction of **Wrigley Field,** home of the Chicago Cubs begins. *(Photo next page.)*

1945 — As the Third Reich crumbled, Hitler's designated successor Herman **Göring sends a telegram to the Führer asking for permission to take control of Nazi Germany.** Hitler responds by stripping Göring of power and appointing different political successors.

1967 — The Soviet Union launches the **Soyuz 1** spacecraft. The mission is plagued with technical problems and eventually crashes due to parachute failure, killing cosmonaut Vladimir Komarov in the **first in-flight fatality in the history of spacecraft.**

1985 — The Coca-Cola company releases **New Coke** to overwhelmingly negative response. The original formula Coke is back on the market in under three months.

Wrigley Field in 1922 (Chicago Daily News)

Soyuz 1 Mission Patch

Quote of the Day

"A pessimist is a man who thinks all women are bad. An optimist is a man who hopes they are."

Chauncey Depew
railroad executive and US senator
born April 23, 1834

Births
and
Deaths

April 23

Singer-songwriter Roy Orbison, born April 23, 1936

Notable April 23 People

With the current world population at about seven billion people, on average about 19 million people also celebrate their birthdays on April 23 — and that isn't counting the millions and millions who came before! No matter when you were born, you share your birthday with many special people whose accomplishments (and occasionally embarrassments) have been noted as part of history.

In this section, you'll meet fascinating people who share your birthday. They're organized by what they're famous for, and then in reverse chronological order from most recent to earliest. Those who are shown in photographs or artwork have a box around them. We don't have photos of everyone, so please forgive us if your favorite person is missing.

Some of these people you've heard of, others may be new to you, but they all make up an important part of the reason that April 23 is a truly special day!

James Buchanan, 15th US President, by John Henry Brown (1851)

Who Was Born on April 23?

Business and Economics

Halston, American fashion designer who created the famous pillbox hat worn by First Lady Jacqueline Kennedy at her husband's presidential inauguration. *(1932)*

Bertil Ohlin, Swedish economist who shared the 1977 Nobel Memorial Prize in Economic Sciences for his research in the theory of international trade. *(1899)*

Crime and Punishment

Timothy McVeigh, domestic terrorist executed for the detonation of a truck bomb in front of an Oklahoma City federal office building. *(1968)*

Government and Military

Bernadette Devlin, controversial Irish republican activist and member of Parliament. *(1947)*

Oleg Penkovsky (Олег Пеньковский), Soviet intelligence colonel who spied on his government on behalf of the United Kingdom and the United States; provided critical information to the West during the Cuban Missile Crisis. *(1919)*

Lester B. Pearson, won the 1957 Nobel Peace Prize for his efforts to resolve the Suez Canal Crisis; later Prime Minister of Canada. *(1897)*

Field Marshal Edmund Allenby, British commander and colonial governor primarily in North Africa known as the commanding officer of T. E. Lawrence ("Lawrence of Arabia") during World War I. *(1861)*

Stephen A. Douglas, Illinois politician best known for his unsuccessful campaign against Abraham Lincoln in the 1860 US Presidential election. *(1813)*

James Buchanan, 15th President of the United States, immediate predecessor of Abraham Lincoln. *(1791)* *(Photo page 22.)*

Abraham Lincoln and **Stephen A. Douglas**

Journalism and Literature

J. P. Donleavy, novelist and playwright whose breakthrough novel was 1955's *The Ginger Man.* *(1926)*

Avram Davidson, critically acclaimed author and editor in science fiction, fantasy, and mysteries

Halldór Laxness, Icelandic writer who received the 1955 Nobel Prize in Literature, the only Icelander to win a Nobel Prize. *(1902)*

Ngaio Marsh, mystery writer best known for her books featuring Inspector Roderick Alleyn. *(1895)*

Music

Steve Clark, guitarist and principal songwriter for the rock band Def Leppard. *(1960)*

Dale Houston, half of the rock duo Dale & Grace whose #1 hit was "I'm Leaving it Up to You." *(1940)*

Roy Orbison, singer-songwriter whose best known hits include "Only the Lonely" and "Oh, Pretty Woman," member of the Rock and Roll Hall of Fame and the Songwriters Hall of Fame. *(1936) (Photo page 20.)*

Cow Cow Davenport, boogie-woogie and piano blues player who inspired the 1943 hit "Cow-Cow Boogie." *(1894)*

Sergei Prokofiev (Сергей Прокофьев), Russian composer whose best known works include the Romeo and Juliet and *Peter and the Wolf*. *(1891)*

Ruggero Leoncavallo, opera composer and librettist whose best known works are the opera *Pagliacci* and the song "Mattinata," made popular by Enrico Caruso. *(1857)*

Science and Medicine

Ray Tomlinson, computer programmer who implemented the first email system and the use of the "@" sign to separate user name from server, member of the Internet Hall of Fame. *(1941)*

Johannes Fibiger, Danish researcher who won the 1926 Nobel Prize in Physiology or Medicine for his cancer research. *(1867)*

Max Planck, German theoretical physicist known as an originator of quantum theory, for which he won the 1918 Nobel Prize in Physics. *(1858)*

Sports

Yelena Shushunova (Елена Шушунова), Russian gymnast who won the gymnastic Grand Slam: Olympics, World Championships, and European/ Continental Championships. *(1969)*

Terry Gordy, professional wrestler who held numerous championship titles, member of the WWE Hall of Fame. *(1961)*

Tony Esposito, ice hockey goaltender for the Chicago Black Hawks, brother of hockey player Phil Esposito, member of the Hockey Hall of Fame. *(1943)*

Gail Goodrich, played basketball for the Los Angeles Lakers and UCLA, named to the Naismith Memorial Basketball Hall of Fame. *(1943)*

Jim Fixx, popularized the health benefits of regular jogging, wrote the 1977 best-seller *The Complete Book of Running. (1932)*

Warren Spahn, pitcher who won the 1957 Cy Young Award; elected to the Baseball Hall of Fame. *(1921)*

Jim Bottomley, first baseman for the St. Louis Cardinals, Cincinnati Reds, and St. Louis Browns; member of the Baseball Hall of Fame. *(1900)*

Television and Film

Kal Penn, best known for playing Kumar Patel in the *Harold & Kumar* film series, served in the Obama White House Office of Public Engagement. (1977)

John Oliver, comedian, television host and political commentator, host of the HBO show *Last Week Tonight with John Oliver. (1977)*

Melina Kankaredes, actress known for her daytime drama role on *Guiding Light,* and for roles in *Providence* and *CSI: NY. (1967)*

John Hannah, Scottish actor best known to international audiences for his role in the 1994 film *Four Weddings and a Funeral,* for which he received a BAFTA nomination.

George Lopez, actor, comedian, and talk show host known for his eponymous sitcom *George Lopez.* *(1961)*

Valerie Bertinelli, actress best known for roles on *One Day at a Time* and *Touched by an Angel,* once married to rocker Eddie Van Halen. *(1960)*

Jan Hooks, actress and comedienne best known for her work on *Saturday Night Live* and *Designing Women.* *(1957)*

Judy Davis, award-winning actress known for such films as *A Passage to India, Absolute Power, Deconstructing Harry,* and *The Dressmaker.* *(1955)*

Michael Moore, documentary filmmaker whose breakthrough 1989 film *Roger & Me* led to other politically-themed documentaries such as the Academy Award-winning *Bowling for Columbine* and *Fahrenheit 9/11,* the highest grossing documentary in American history. *(1954)*

Blair Brown, actress known for the title role in the television series *The Days and Nights of Molly Dodd,* and for supporting roles in *Fringe* and *Orange is the New Black.* *(1946)*

Hervé Villechaize, actor who first became famous as Tattoo in the television series *Fantasy Island,* who exclaimed "Ze plane! Ze plane!" at the beginning of each episode; played the villain Nick Nack in the Bond film *The Man With the Golden Gun.* *(1943)*

Sandra Dee

Hervé Villechaize (with Ricardo Montalban)

Sandra Dee, model and actress famous for roles in two 1959 films, *Imitation of Life* and *Gidget;* wife of singer Bobby Darin; subject of the *Grease* song "Look at Me, I'm Sandra Dee." *(1942) (Photo previous page.)*

Lee Majors, actor who starred in *The Six Million Dollar Man* and *The Fall Guy. (1939)*

Shirley Temple, child actress who was Hollywood's number one box-office star in the late 1930s, famous for such films as *Curly Top, Little Miss Marker*, and *Bright Eyes*, later a US Ambassador and Chief of Protocol. *(1928)*

Simone Simon, French actress best known for such films as *The Devil and Daniel Webster* (1941), *Cat People* (1942), and many more. *(1910)*

Duncan Renaldo, actor best known for his portrayal of the Cisco Kid in films and on television. *(1904)*

Duncan Renaldo as The Cisco Kid, with his horse Diablo

Shirley Temple (with Arthur Treacher) in *The Little Princess*

Howard Cosell, sportscaster. Cosell died April 23, 1995.

Who Died on April 23?

Business and Economics

Paul Erdman, best-selling writer on business and finance, wrote several novels involving international finance, including the Edgar Award-winning *The Billion Dollar Sure Thing. (2007)*

Crime and Punishment

James Earl Ray, assassin of Martin Luther King, Jr. *(1998)*

Government and Politics

Boris Yeltsin (Борис Ельцин), first president of post-Soviet Russia. *(2007)*

Cesar Chavez, labor leader and civil rights activist who founded the United Farm Workers union. *(1993)*

Sam Ervin, US senator from North Carolina best known for leading the Senate investigating committee during the Watergate scandal. *(1985)*

Charles G. Dawes, US Vice President under Calvin Coolidge, shared the 1925 Nobel Peace Prize for his work on the Dawes Plan for World WarI reparations. *(1951)*

Boris Godunov (Бори́с Годуно́в), ruler of Russia as regent and later tsar from 1585 to 1605, best known as the subject of the opera of the same name. *(1605‡)*

Æthelred the Unready, King of the English from 978 to 1016. "Unready" is a mistranslation of the Old English *unræd*, meaning "ill-advised," for ordering the St. Brice's Day massacre of Danish settlers, whih resulted in a Danish invasion of England. *(1016)*

Brian Boru, High King of Ireland considered to have unified the island, ancestor of US President John F Kennedy. *(1014)*

Journalism and Literature

David Halberstam, historian and journalist who won a Pulitzer Prize for International Reporting; his best-selling books include *The Best and the Brightest* and *The Powers That Be. (2007)*

P. L. Travers, novelist best known for the *Mary Poppins* books. *(1996)*

Rupert Brooke, English poet known for his war sonnets about World War I, especially "The Soldier." *(1915)*

---

‡ He died on April 23 according to the Gregorian calendar, used in most of Europe. His birthday in the "Old Style" (OS) Julian calendar is April 13. For an explanation of different calendar types, see "What Day of the Week is April 23?"

Boris Godunov

William Wordsworth, major English poet of the Romantic era whose best known works include "I Wandered Lonely as a Cloud" and "The World is Too Much With Us." *(1850)*

William Shakespeare, poet and playwright generally considered the greatest writer in the English language. *(1616)*

Military and Exploration

Alferd[§] **Packer,** American prospector famous for resorting to cannibalism while stranded in the mountains of Colorado, subject of the biopic *The Legend of Alfred Packer* and the play *Cannibal! The Musical. (1850)*

Music

Harold Arlen, Great American Songbook composer who wrote the songs for the 1939 The Wizard of Oz, including "Over the Rainbow;" other hits include "Get Happy," "It's Only a Paper Moon," and "Stormy Weather." *(1986)*

Red Garland, jazz pianist best known for his work with the Miles Davis Quintet. *(1984)*

[§] Although his given name was "Alfred," he spelled it "Alferd."

Title page of the "First Folio" of William Shakespeare's plays (1623)

Religion

Margaret Fell, early Quaker preacher and missionary known as the "mother of Quakerism." *(1702)*

Science and Medicine

George Ohsawa, founded the Macrobiotic diet and philosophy using Oriental concepts of health. *(1966)*

George Adamski, "ufologist" who claimed to have photographed spaceships from other planets and met with friendly space aliens; two of his books became best sellers. *(1965)*

Sports

Dennis Compton, cricketer for Middlesex, named to the Cricket Hall of Fame in 2009. *(1997)*

Howard Cosell, legendary television sportscaster. *(1995)* *(Photo page 32.)*

Television and Fllm

John Mills, actor who received an Academy Award for his performance in the 1970 film *Ryan's Daughter;* co starred with his daughter Hayley Mills in *The Truth About Spring* and *The Chalk Garden. (2005)*

Satyajit Ray (সত্যজিৎ রায়), Indian filmmaker considered one of the greatest of the 20th century, particurlarly known for *Pather Panchali* and *The Apu Trilogy. (1992)*

Paulette Goddard, actress known for her roles in such films as *Modern Times* (with Charlie Chaplin), *Second Chorus* (with Fred Astaire), and *Kitty. (1990)*

Otto Preminger, directed such films as *Laura, The Man with the Golden Arm*, and *Anatomy of a Murder. (1986)*

Buster Crabbe, Olympic gold medal swimmer best known as an actor for his roles in the serials *Flash Gordon* and *Buck Rogers. (1983)*

William Hartnell, English actor best known for playing the first incarnation of the Doctor in the long-running tv series *Doctor Who. (1975)*

Buster Crabbe

Quote of the Day

"I stopped believing in Santa Claus when I was six. Mother took me to see him in a department store and he asked for my autograph."

Shirley Temple, child actress and diplomat
born April 23, 1928

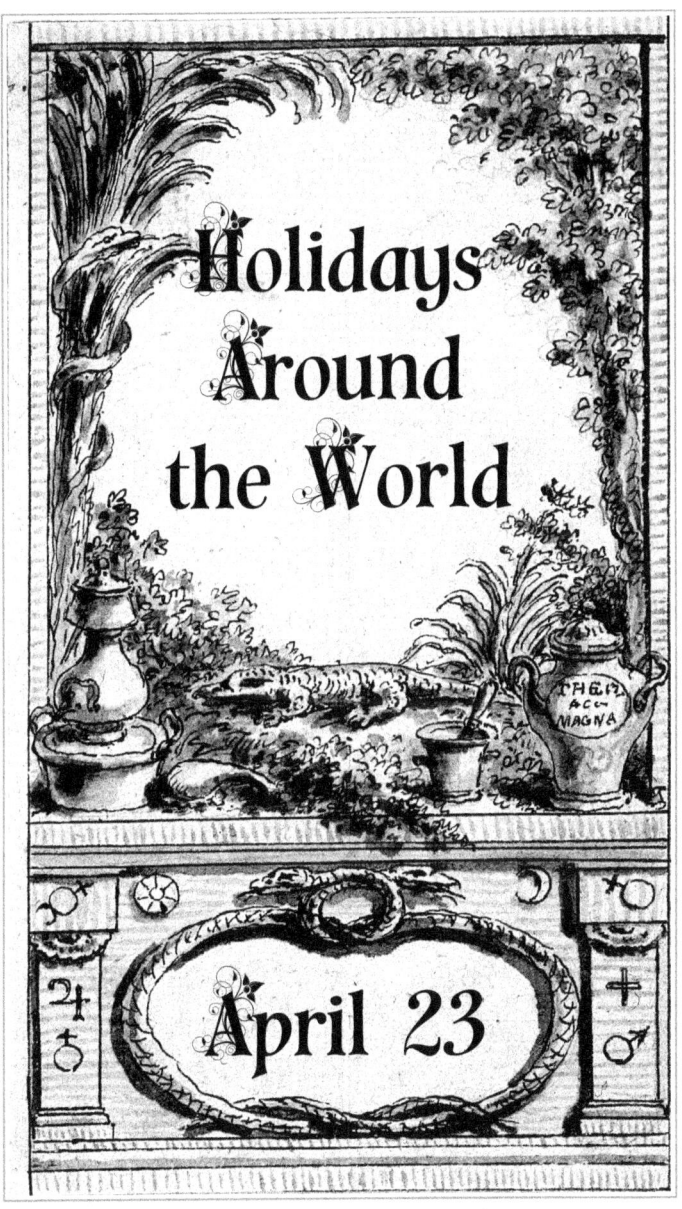

Holidays
Around
the World

April 23

The Picnic, by Eugen Klimsch (1894), for NATIONAL PICNIC DAY

Holidays Around the World

If you're looking for a reason to take your special day off, you should know that every single day is a holiday somewhere in the world! Here's some of what you can celebrate on April 23!

General Events

Castile and León Day in that region of Spain commemorates the Battle of Villalar on April 23, 1521.

English Language Day is one of six days dedicated to the six official working languages of the United Nations. The date was chosen because of its association with William Shakespeare.

Independence Day in the "Conch Republic," an humorous "secession" of Key West from the United States, declared on April 23, 1982.

Khongjom Day in the former Kingdom **of Manipur (India)** commemorates the April 23, 1891, Battle of Khongjom, a key event in the Anglo-Manipur War.

Many nations set aside one or more days to honor their armed forces. **Navy Day** in the **People's Republic of China** celebrates its navy on April 23.

Ulusal Egemenlik ve Çocuk Bayramı (National Sovereignty Day and Children's Day) in Turkey and Northern Cyprus. On the occasion of the Grand National Assembly of Turkey declaring an independent modern republic, founder Kemal Ataturk made a present of April 23 to all the world's children, so April 23 is both Turkish National Sovereignty Day, and a worldwide Children's Day.

World Book Day, created by UNESCO, promotes reading, writing, and copyright. It began on April 23, 1995.

Celebrations About Food

In the United States, almost every day of the year is dedicated to a particular food. (Some other countries also have official food days, but only in America is there one every single day!) Sponsored by manufacturers, retailers, farmers, or simply fans, these days are often proclaimed by the President, Congress, state governors, or mayors. Given that there are more different foods than days of the year, some days honor more than one kind of food!

Some foods just get a day, while others get a whole month. Here's what to eat on April 23 and the rest of the month of April!

April 23 is both **National Cherry Cheescake Day** and **National Picnic Day,** so be sure to put some in your picnic basket. *(Photo page 42.)*

The whole month of April is set aside to honorthe following foods.

- National Florida Tomato Month
- National BLT Sandwich Month

- National Pecan Month
- National Soft Pretzel Month
- National Soyfoods Month
- National Grilled Cheese Month
- National Garlic Month

Honorary Months

Presidents, Congresses, and nations around the world issue proclamations recognizing particular months to honor certain causes. These events generally fall in April, though honorary months do come and go.

Holidays established by states and nonprofit organizations are listed if verified. If not otherwise specified, all months are US. There is some variation from year to year; some celebratory months get added and others get dropped. Two places to get up to date information are the current edition of Chase's Calendar of Events *or the website Brownielocks. Here are some honorary designations for April.*

- Alcohol Awareness Month (National Council on Alcoholism and Drug Dependence)
- Cancer Control Month
- Confederate History Month (Alabama, Florida, Georgia, Louisiana, Mississippi, Texas, Virginia)
- Earthquake Preparedness Month (California)
- Fair Housing Month
- Grange Month (National Grange)
- Holy Humor Month (Fellowship of Merry Christians)

- International Guitar Month
- Jazz Appreciation Month (Smithsonian Institution)
- Month of the Young Child® (Michigan Association for the Education of Young Children)
- National Arab-American Heritage Month
- National Autism Awareness Month (Autism Society of America)
- National Car Care Month (Car Care Council)
- National Child Abuse Prevention Month
- National Donate Life Month (Organ donations)
- National Frog Month
- National Greyhound Adoption Month
- National Kite Month (American Kiteflyers Association)
- National Landscape Architecture Month (American Society of Landscape Architects)
- National Occupational Therapy Month
- National Poetry Month (Academy of American Poets)
- National Poetry Writing Month (NaPoWriMo)
- National Youth Sports Safety Month (National Youth Sports Safety Foundation)
- Parkinson's Disease Awareness Month (International)
- Prevention of Animal Cruelty Month (ASPCA)
- School Library Media Month (American Library Association)

- Sexual Assault Awareness and Prevention Month (National Sexual Violence Resource Center)
- Sports Eye Safety Month (American Academy of Ophthalmology)
- Straw Hat Month

Moveable and Multi-Day Events

Some events take place over a specific week or time period. Start and finish dates may vary from year to year. Some events occur on different days each year (such as "fourth Saturday of a month"). These events sometimes take place on April 23.

Third Week of April

The third week in April can begin on April 9 and end as late as April 21. The third Monday or Friday of that week can be as early as April 15 or as late as April 23.

- National Coin Week (American Numismatic Association)
- National Library Week (American Library Association)
- National Volunteer Week (Points of Light Foundation)
- National Wildlife Week (National Wildlife Federation)
- Occupational Health Nurses Week (American Association of Occupational Health Nurses; usually third week but always in April)

- Week of the Young Child (Association for the Education of Young Children)

Fourth Week of April

The fourth week of April can begin on April 22 and end as late as April 30. In most months, the fourth week in April is also the last, but occasionally April goes to a fifth week, consisting of the 30th and sometimes the 29th as well.

- Administrative Professionals Week (last full week in April, International Association of Administrative Professionals; Administrative Professionals Day is the Wednesday of that week)
- National Infant Immunization Week (last week in April, sometimes overlapping into the first few days of May)
- National Playground Safety Week

Last Saturday in April

The last Saturday in April can be any day from April 23 to April 29.

- Children's Day (Colombia)

Just for Fun

Anybody can make up a holiday, and many people do! While none of these are officially recognized and some may come and go, here are a few more holidays for April 23.

- Impossible Astronaut Day (for *Doctor Who* fans)
- International Pixel-Stained Technopeasant Day

- Movie Theater Day
- Talk Like Shakespeare Day

Religious Feast Days and Holidays

Every religion normally has feast days and holidays associated with it. While some religious days take place on a given calendar day, others occur on different days each year, usually because the date is determined by the phases of the Moon rather than the Earth's path around the Sun. Here are some religious feasts, festivals, and holidays that sometimes or always fall on April 23! (For Easter season events, see the following chapter.)

Passover (פסח) (Judaism, Samaritanism, Saint Thomas Christians)

Passover commemorates the liberation of the Israelites from slavery in ancient Egypt around 3,300 years ago. Its story is told in the Biblical book of Exodus, which is part of both the Jewish and Samaritan Torahs and the Christian Old Testament. Exodus tells how God inflicted ten plagues upon the ancient Egyptians before the Pharaoh would release its slaves. The tenth plague killed every Egyptian first-born child. Israelites marked the doorposts of their homes with the blood of a spring lamb so that the spirit of the Lord would "pass over" the first-born in those homes. Passover is celebrated by Jews in a festive ritual dinner known as a Seder and by Samaritans with an animal sacrifice on Mount Gerizim.

For most celebrants, Passover begins on the 15th day of Nisan and ends on the 21st of Nisan in Israel and on the 22nd of Nisan outside of Israel. The earliest dates for Passover are between March 21 and March 27 (or 28), and the latest dates fall between April 20 and April 26 (or 27).

A children's Passover seder

Saint George's Day (numerous nations)

Saint George's Day celebrations are common in many nations in Europe and the Middle East. Not all of them fall on the same day.

- In Western Christian churches, if April 23 falls during Holy Week or on Easter Day, the celebration is automatically moved to the Monday after the Second Sunday of Easter.

- In the Czech Republic, Saint George's Day is celebrated on April 24 to avoid conflict with the feast day of St. Adalbert of Prague, that country's national saint.

- In many Orthodox Christian countries, St. George's Day is celebrated on May 6, the Julian** equivalent of April 23.
- Palestinians hold a feast for Al-Khidr, the Muslim equivalent of St. George, on May 5.

Vesak (वैशाख) (Buddhism)

Vesak, sometimes written as Vesākha or Wesak, commemorates the birth, enlightenment, and death of Gautama Buddha, and is sometimes informally called "Buddha's Birthday." Vesak takes its name from the Asian lunisolar month of Vaisakha, and because its date comes from a different calendar, it takes place on varying dates in the Western (Gregorian) calendar, usually in April or May, although in leap years it can be celebrated in June.

On Vesak, Buddhists attend ceremonies in their local temples to sing hymns and bring offerings of flowers, candles, and joss-sticks. They typically eat only vegetarian food on that day. Birds, insects, and other animals are released in large numbers as a symbolic act of liberation. Devout Buddhists devote the day to charitable acts and to decorating their temples, and to work at following the Buddha's teachings.

In Japan, the festival is known as *Hana Matsuri* (花祭), and is always celebrated on April 8.

** For an explanation of different calendar types, see "What Day of the Week is April 23?"

Saint Days

Each day in the year is considered a feast day for one or more saints. They are somewhat different in western Christianity (Catholicism and many forms of Protestantism) and in eastern (Orthodox) Christianity. The list of saints, martyrs, and others is quite extensive, so not all are necessarily listed.

In **Western Christianity,** April 23 is the feast day of Saints Adalbert of Prague, George, Gerard of Toul, and Toyohiko Kagawa (Episcopal and Lutheran churches).

In **Eastern Orthodox Christianity,** it is also the commemoration of Saints Marolus, Ibar of Beggerin, and Pusinna. (These saints are honored on April 10 by Old Calendrists.[††])

[††] "Old Calendrists" use the Julian, rather than the Gregorian, calendar. For an explanation of different calendar types, see "What Day of the Week is April 23?"

Easter Season

La crucifixion by El Greco

The Christian holiday of Easter in Western Christianity is held on the first Sunday after the Paschal Full Moon following the March equinox, which is officially set at March 21 by church reckoning. Easter itself can therefore occur as early as March 22 and as late as April 25, but occurs most often in April. In Eastern Christianity, which uses the Julian calendar[‡‡] for liturgical purposes, Easter occurs between April 4 and May 8. This also sets the date for the various events that lead up to Easter, most importantly the events of Holy Week.

Passion Sunday

The fifth Sunday of the Christian season of Lent is known as Passion Sunday in various Protestant denominations and by some traditionalist Catholics. Passion Sunday starts the two-week Passiontide, which ends on Holy Saturday, the day before Easter, commemorating the day that Jesus's body was laid in the tomb. The fifth Sunday of Lent can occur as early as March 8 (though the next time it will be that early is in 2285 CE), and as late as April 11.

Palm Sunday

The moveable feast of Palm Sunday commemorates the triumphant entry of Jesus into Jerusalem, an event mentioned in all four gospels. In many Christian churches, palm leaves are distributed to the worshippers. The earliest date for Palm Sunday is March 15, and the latest is April 18.

[‡‡] For an explanation of different calendar types, see "What Day of the Week is April 23?"

Maundy Thursday

The Thursday before Easter is Maundy Thursday, when the Last Supper took place. Because of its relation to Easter, the earliest day it can occur is March 19, and the latest it can occur is April 22.

Good Friday

Good Friday, observed during Holy Week on the Friday preceding Easter Sunday, commemorates the crucifixion of Jesus and his death at Calvary. Because of its relation to Easter, the earliest day it can occur is March 20, and the latest it can occur is April 23.

Holy Saturday

Sometimes called Easter Eve or Black Saturday, Holy Saturday commemorates the day in which Jesus's body lay in the tomb. Some mistakenly refer to this day as "Easter Saturday," but that properly describes the Saturday following Easter, the last day of Easter Week. The earliest it can occur is March 21, and the latest it can occur is April 24.

Easter Day

Easter celebrates the resurrection of Jesus Christ on the third day after his crucifixion. In the liturgical calendar, Easter follows the season of Lent, and begins the period known as Eastertide, which ends on Pentecost Sunday.

Easter is observed religiously in a morning service. In the U.S., it's also common to decorate

Easter eggs and make Easter baskets of eggs and
candy, often with the Easter bunny as a symbol. The
White House traditionally hosts an egg hunt, and
many communities have Easter parades.

Easter customs around the world include bonfires
(Cyprus, western Sweden), men spanking women
with a ceremonial whip (Czech Republic and
Slovakia), egg fighting (Bulgaria), cross-country
skiing and reading murder mysteries (Norway), and
children dressed as witches collecting candy door-to-
door (other Nordic countries).

Easter Eggs

Easter Monday

In some Roman Catholic and Eastern Orthodox
cultures, the Monday after Easter is celebrated as a
holiday. It is also known as Egg Nyte, featuring egg

rolling competitions and dousing other people with water that had been blessed with holy water the previous day at mass. Easter Monday is also celebrated as Family Day in South Africa. In Guyana, people fly kites that were made on Holy Saturday. In Portugal, it is known as the *Anjo* (Ivy) Festival, in which people picnic in the countryside.

Śmigus-Dyngus (Poland, Hungary, Czech Republic, Slovakia)

The Monday after Easter in Poland and in the Polish diaspora is known as *Śmigus-Dyngus*, or simply Dyngus Day in the US. Boys throw water over girls they like and spank them with pussy willows. Girls avoid getting wet by giving boys "ransoms" of painted eggs.

Easter Week (Western Christianity), Bright Week (Eastern Christianity)

The period from Easter Sunday to the following Saturday is known as Easter Week. In both Western and Eastern Christianity (where it's known as Bright Week), the resurrection continues to be celebrated in church services. Easter Tuesday is a public holiday in the Australian state of Tasmania.

Egg Salad Week (American Egg Board)

Egg Salad Week celebrates the many ways to use all the Easter eggs gathered on the holiday, normally celebrated the week following Easter Sunday.

Quote of the Day

"If April showers
Should come your way,
They bring the flowers
That bloom in May."

from the song "April Showers" (1921)
lyrics by Buddy DeSylva, music by Louis Silvers

About
the
Month
of

April

THEM
ACC
MAGNA

"April," from the *Brevarium Grimani* by Simon Bening (c.1510)

April: The Fourth Month

"I love the season well
When forest glades are teeming with bright forms,
Nor dark and many-folded clouds foretell
The coming on of storms."
           — *"An April Day,"* Henry Wadsworth Longfellow

The origin of the name "April" (Latin: *Aprilis*) for the fourth month of the year is uncertain. Some say that it comes from the Latin verb *aperire*, meaning "to open," a reference to springtime. A similar word in Greek, ἄνοιξις (*anoixis*, meaning "opening") also refers to spring.

On the other hand, the Romans named many months after their gods, such as "January" for Janus and "March" (*Martius*) for Mars. The month of April was sacred to the goddess Venus (Aphrodite in Greek), and thus some think that April refers to her.

The fairy tale collector Jacob Grimm suggested that April came from the Etruscan name Apru, and believed that an Etruscan god or hero of that name gave rise to the month.

The Anglo-Saxons called April *Oster-monath*, sometimes spelled *Eostur-monath*, named for the goddess Eostre. The Venerable Bede, a monk who wrote the first history of the English people, argued that Eostur was the root of the word Easter.

As the original Roman calendar started its new year in March, April was originally the second month of the year. It's uncertain when the Romans switched the new year to January, but it may have been as late as 153 BCE.

April is the springtime month in the northern hemisphere and fall in the southern hemisphere; October is its opposite. It's one of only four calendar months with thirty days. Originally, April had only 29 days, but the calendar reforms of Julius Caesar (the Julian Calendar) added the 30th day.

The first day of April and the first day of July always fall on the same day of the week; in leap years the first of January also falls on the same weekday as the first of April. In all years, the last day of April and the last day of December fall on the same weekday.

The Jewish month of Nisan (נִיסָן) overlaps with March and the first part of April. Months in Islam and Hindi culture operate on a lunar cycle, and so the months slowly migrate through the year.

April in Other Cultures

The month of April has different names in different languages. Some nations use calendars other than the Gregorian, and their months may overlap with April. Still, they often have a word for April itself.

Albanian: Prill

Arabic (Egypt, Sudan, Yemen): مارأبريل (Abrīl)

Belarussian: красавік (Krasavik)

Bulgarian: април (April)

Chinese (Mandarin): 四月 (Sìyuè)

Croatian: Travanj

Czech: Duben

Finnish: Huhtikuu (burnwood month)

French: Avril

Greek: Απρίλιος (Aprílios)

Hebrew: אפריל (Âprîl)

Hindi: अप्रैल (Aprail)

Irish (Gaelic): Aibreán mí Aibreáin

Italian: Aprile

Japanese: 四月 (Shigatsu)

Korean: 사월 (Saweol)

Lithuanian: Balandis

Old English: Ēastermōnaþ

Polish: Kwiecień

Russian: апрель (Aprel')

Scots: Apryle

Scottish Gaelic: an Giblean

Swahili: Aprili

Thai: เมษายน (Mesayon)

Ukrainian: квітень (Kviten')

Vietnamese: Tháng tư

April Sayings and Superstitions

Here are some sayings and superstitions associated with the month of April.

- "April showers bring May flowers."
- "If early April is foggy / Rain in June will make lanes boggy."
- "When April blows its horn / 'Tis good for hay and corn."
- "April wet — good wheat."
- "Till April's dead, change not a thread."
- "Marry in May and rue the day, but marry in April if you can, joy for maiden and for man."

Which day to get married? That's easy. "Monday for wealth, Tuesday for health, Wednesday the best day of all, Thursday for losses, Friday for crosses, Saturday for no luck at all."

April Symbols

Birthstone Diamond

Diamond

Birth Flowers Daisy and Sweet Pea

Daisy

Sweet Pea

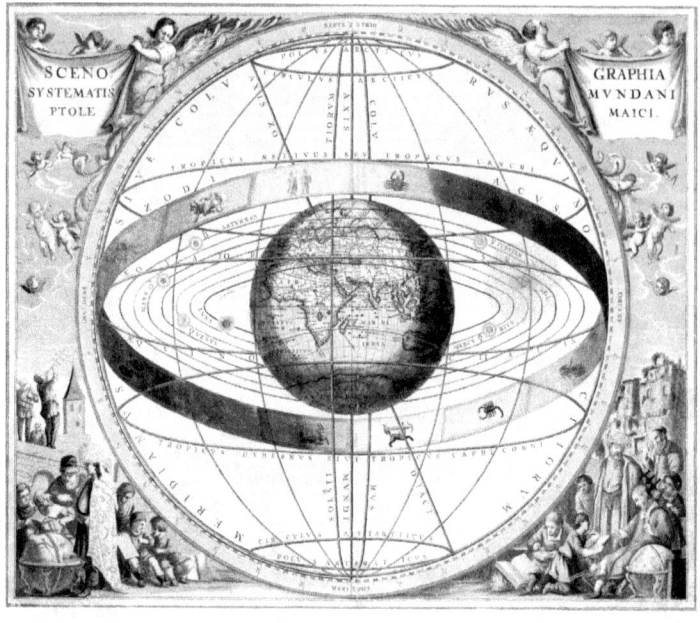

Scenography of the Ptolemaic Cosmography, by Johannes van
Loon, based on Andreas Cellarius's *Harmonia Macrocosmica,* 1660

April 23 Zodiac Signs

From the perspective of someone on Earth, the Sun appears to move through the sky throughout the year, along a path astronomers call the *ecliptic plane*. The ecliptic plane is divided into twelve constellations, known as the zodiac, based on traditionally observed patterns of stars. On your birthday, you can't see your constellation, because it's in the daytime sky.

The zodiac was first developed by Babylonian astronomers about 2,500 years ago. Because they were unaware that the Earth wobbles like a spinning top (known as *precession*), they didn't make allowance for the fact that the Sun's path through the zodiac changes over time.

That means there are now two sets of dates for your birth sign. The *tropical dates* are the original Babylonian dates; the *sidereal dates* tell you where the Sun actually appears as it moves along its annual path.

For April 23, the tropical sign is **Taurus** and the sidereal sign is **Capricorn.**

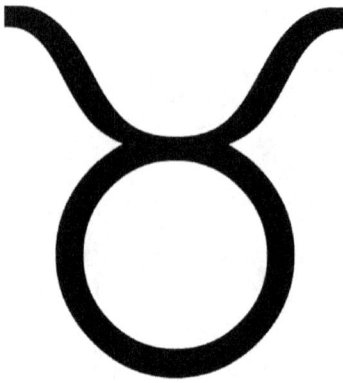

Taurus

Tropical April 21 to May 22
Siderial May 16 to June 15

In Greek mythology, Taurus was a disguise adopted by Zeus, who appeared to the maiden Europa in the form of a gentle white bull. Europa unwisely got too close, and Zeus kidnapped her to the island of Crete, where she bore him three sons, including Minos, builder of the labyrinth that housed the minotaur.

In astrology, Taurus is an earth sign, and Taureans are supposed to be quiet, gentle, compassionate, and stubborn. Taureans can appreciate the finer things in life and are cautious with money.

Aries

Tropical March 21 to April 19
Sidereal April 15 to May 15

In Greek mythology, Aries is a ram with golden wings and golden wool who rescued the twins Phrixus and Helle from certain death. Although Helle died in the rescue attempt, the grateful Phrixus sacrificed the ram to Zeus. The golden fleece from the sacrificed ram played a prominent part in the later myth of Jason and the Argonauts.

In astrology, Aries, a fire sign, is compatible with the other fire signs of Gemini, Leo, and Sagittarius, and to a lesser extent with air signs Scorpio and Libra. Arians are supposed to be adventurous, enthusiastic, quick-tempered, and impulsive.

Illustration by Edward Penfield

What Day of the Week is April 23?

On what day of the week does April 23 fall?

Surprisingly, this isn't an easy question. Because the calendar year is 365 days long (366 in leap years), it doesn't divide evenly by the seven days of the week.

Also, the Earth goes around the Sun in about 365-1/4 days, so a calendar tends to drift over time. That's why the same date falls on different weekdays in different years.

This is made even more complicated by a change in calendars that took place in 1582. Our modern calendar has its roots in ancient Rome, in a calendar reform conducted by Julius Caesar. Caesar commissioned mathematicians to attack the problem, and they came up with the idea of leap years, and thus standardized the calendar for centuries to come. This was called the Julian calendar.

Over time, however, the small errors in Caesar's calculation compounded. That's why Pope Gregory XIII commissioned the Gregorian calendar, used in most of the world today. Some countries converted in 1582, when the calendar was first developed; some converted later; other still haven't changed.

Gregorian and Julian aren't the only types of calendars. The Hebrew year, the Islamic year, and many other calendars are used in different parts of the world and among different people.

You can convert Gregorian dates to other calendars, including the Hebrew calendar, the Islamic calendar, and even the Mayan calendar by visiting the Fourmilab Calendar Converter at http://www.fourmilab.ch/documents/calendar/.

Chinese calendar systems are quite complex and have changed several times; a full discussion is far beyond the scope of this book. If you're interested, you can find information here: http://www.hermetic.ch/cal_stud/chinese_cal.htm.

On Names and Dates

Historians use "CE" (Common Era) and "BCE" (Before the Common Era) instead of the more common "AD" (Anno Domini, or Year of Our Lord) and "BC" (Before Christ), reflecting the fact that the year-numbering system established by the Gregorian calendar is used throughout the world in many countries not culturally Christian.

The CE/BCE designation dates back to at least 1708, and has been adopted as a standard by the United Nations and the Universal Postal Union. Because this series of books covers events and people of all nations and cultures, we use the CE/BCE terms.

The abbreviation "O.S." ("Old Style") and "N.S." ("New Style") on some dates refers to the fact that the Russian Empire (in particular) did not switch from the Julian to the Gregorian calendar at the same time as the rest of Europe, and therefore some figures and events have two dates.

Also, in the Julian calendar in England in the 16th century, the year began on March 25 rather than January 1. To avoid confusion with Gregorian dates, dates between January and March were often written using both years.

People and events whose original names are not in the Western alphabet have their native names (where possible) in the appropriate script shown in parenthesis. If you are using an e-reader to access an electronic version of this book, all characters don't always display on all devices.

A 50-year brass perpetual calendar.

Quote of the Day

"Time is an illusion, lunchtime doubly so."

Douglas Adams,
from *The Hitchhiker's Guide to the Galaxy*

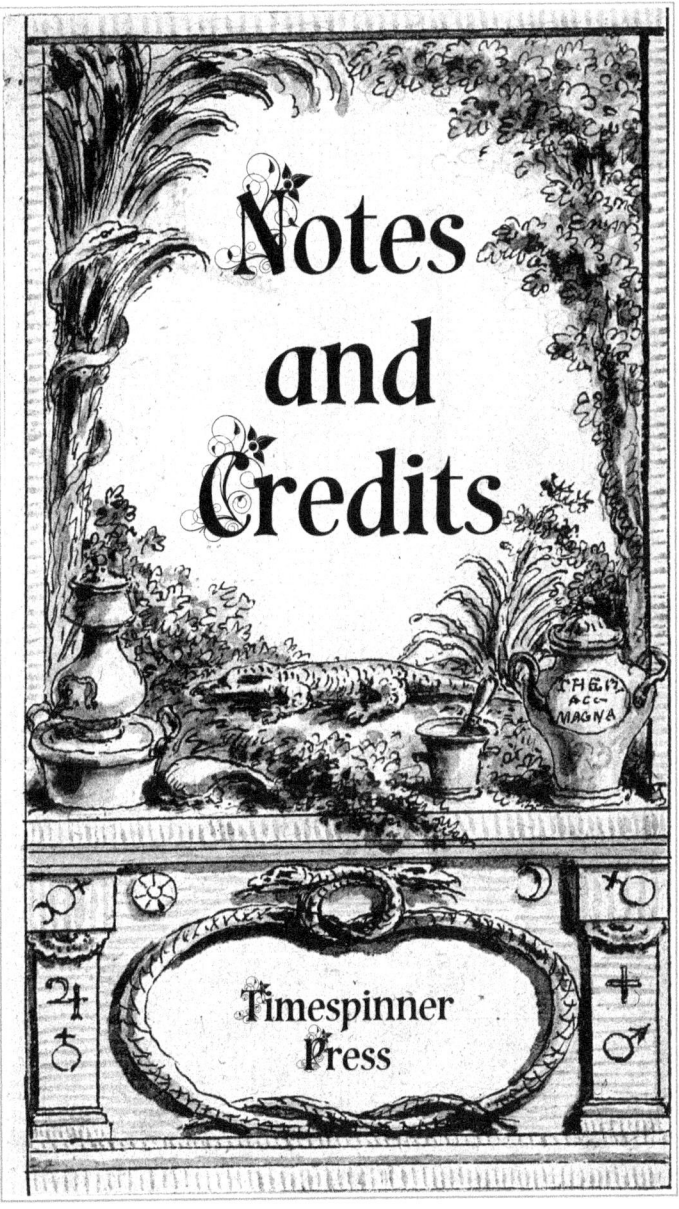

Notes
and
Credits

Timespinner
Press

Cartoon by John T. McCutcheon

Copyright, Credit, and Contact

Follow Us

Our blog "This Day in History" (http://
timespinnerpress.com/this-day-in-history/) features short
articles on events and people associated with each day, and
updates several times each week. Also subscribe to the
"Quote of the Day" at http://timespinnerpress.com/quote-
of-the-day/. You can get daily links by following us on
Facebook at TimespinnerPress, or on Twitter as
@sidewisethinker.

Contact Us

Find an error or a format problem? Want information about
the series, about us, or about when the volume for your
special day might be available? Please email us at
editor@timespinnerpress.com. (We also take requests if your
special day isn't yet complete. Please give us at least six
weeks' notice if possible.)

Sources

We owe a great debt to Wikipedia, which is our first stop for
research. We attempt to make independent confirmation of
all important dates and facts through a variety of other
sources.

Other sources we frequently use include the Library of
Congress; "on this day" listings from *Encyclopedia Britannica*,
the *New York Times*, and the BBC; Omniglot for the names of
months in other languages; *Chase's Calendar of Events*; and, of
course, the always essential Google.

All art and photographs are either in the public domain, used under a Creative Commons license, or with a "fair use" justification, and most frequently come from Wikimedia Commons and the Library of Congress Prints and Photographs Division.

Attribution is provided where possible, or as requested by the copyright owner, or when there is particular historical significance, listed below. For information about any particular illustration or photograph, please contact us.

Credits

1. The cover photograph of a stained glass window of St. George and the Dragon was taken by G. Freihalter in 2010. It is used here under CC BY-SA 3.0.

2. The illustration of the month of April used on the back cover is from the French Gothic illuminated manuscript *Les Très Riches Heures du duc de Berry* by the Limbourg Brothers, Jean Colombe, and an intermediate painter whose name is lost to history. It is in the public domain because its copyright has expired.

3. The box graphic used on the first page is from a 1916 pamphlet entitled "Divorce versus Democracy" authored by G. K. Chesterton, originally published in London by the Society of St. Peter and St. Paul. It is in the public domain in the US because it was published prior to 1923, and is in the public domain in all countries (including the country of origin) in which the copyright time is the author's life plus 70 years or less.

4. The graphic design for the section pages in this book is from a design originally created for a pharmacy label. It is courtesy of Wellcome Images (ICV No 11073, photo V0010813), and is used here under CC BY-SA 4.0.

5. The painting "The Torture of St. George" by Michiel Coxie was created circa 1580, and is in the public domain because its copyright has expired. The original can be found in the Saint Rombout Cathedralin Mechelen, Belgium. The photograph was taken by Michel Wal in 2008, who claims

copyright, although photographs of paintings generally do not qualify for such protection. In any event, the photograph is licensed under CC BY-SA 3.0.

6. The woodcut "Saint George Killing the Dragon" by Albrect Dürer was created between 1501 and 1504, and is in the public domain because its copyright has expired. It is in the collection of the National Gallery of Art, Washington, DC, accession number 1943.3.3597.

7. The photograph of the Union Jack was taken in 2007 by Vaughan Leiberum. It is used here under CC BY-SA 2.0.

8. The engraving "The Fair of Saint George's Day" was created between 1559 and 1562 by Peter Brueghel the Elder, and is in the public domain because its copyright has expired. The original is in the collection of the Museum of Fine Arts, Houston, accession number 97.309.

9. The 1922 rendering of Wrigley Field originally appeared in the Chicago *Daily News*. It is in the public domain because its first publication occurred prior to January 1, 1923.

10. The Soyuz 1 mission patch is not an object of copyright according to article 1259 of Book IV of the Civil Code of the Russian Federation No. 230-FZ of December 18, 2006.

11. The 2012 photograph of a tray of beer served at the Brauereigasthof Rothenbach in Aufseß, Bavaria, Germany, is by Ben Reis, and is used here under CC BY-SA 3.0.

12. The 1965 advertising photograph of Roy Orbison riding a motorcyclefirst appeared in *Billboard* magazine. It is in the public domain because it was published in the United States between 1923 and 1977 and without a copyright notice.

13. The 1851 portrait of James Buchanan by John Henry Brown is in the public domain because its copyright has expired. It is courtesy of the White House Historical Association, accession number 989.1665.1.

14. The composite photograph of Abraham Lincoln and Stephen A. Douglas consists of images taken in 1860 and 1859 respectively, and is in the public domain because both copyrights have expired.

15. The 1961 publicity photograph of Sandra Dee by Universal Studios is in the public domain because it was published in the United States between 1923 and 1977 without a

copyright notice. Traditionally, publicity photographs are not copyrighted because of the way in which they are intended to be used.

16. The 1977 publicity photograph from the made-for-television movie *Return to Fantasy Island* is in the public domain because it was published in the United States between 1923 and 1977 without a copyright notice. Traditionally, publicity photographs are not copyrighted because of the way in which they are intended to be used.

17. The 1953 publicity photograph of the Cisco Kid and his horse Diablo is in the public domain because it was published in the United States between 1923 and 1977 without a copyright notice. Traditionally, publicity photographs are not copyrighted because of the way in which they are intended to be used.

18. The 1939 publicity photograph from the film *The Little Princess* is in the public domain because it was published in the United States between 1923 and 1977 without a copyright notice. Traditionally, publicity photographs are not copyrighted because of the way in which they are intended to be used.

19. The 1975 publicity photograph of Howard Cosell from *Monday Night Football* is in the public domain because it was published in the United States between 1923 and 1977 without a copyright notice. Traditionally, publicity photographs are not copyrighted because of the way in which they are intended to be used.

20. The artist who created the 17th century portrait of Boris Godunov is unknown. The image is in the public domain because its copyright has expired.

21. The 1936 publicity photograph of of Buster Crabbe as Flash Gordon is in the public domain because it was published in the United States between 1923 and 1977 without a copyright notice. Traditionally, publicity photographs are not copyrighted because of the way in which they are intended to be used.

22. The 1894 painting *Das Picknick* by Eugen Klimsch is in the public domain because its copyright has expired.

23. The photograph of a passover seder table was taken in the Ahawah Children's Home, Berlin; it is free of any known copyright restrictions. Image from the Center for Jewish History, New York, New York.

24. The painting *La Crucifixión* by El Greco is located in the Museo del Prado. It is in the public domain because its copyright has expired.

25. The photograph of Czechoslovakian Easter eggs was taken by Jan Kameníček, who has released the image into the public domain.

26. The painting "April" is from the *Brevarium Grimani*, circa 1510, and is in the public domain because its copyright has expired.

27. The photograph of two diamonds grown by Washington Diamonds was taken by Inbai-Tania Studio, and is used here under the CC BY-SA 3.0 license.

28. The photograph of a daisy (*Bellis perennis*) was taken by André Karwath and is used here under the CC BY-SA 2.5 license.

29. The 1815 woodcut of a proposal is in the public domain because its copyright has expired.

30. The celestial sphere is from *Scenography of the Ptolemaic Cosmography*, by Johannes van Loon, based on Andreas Cellarius's *Harmonia Macrocosmica*, 1660. It is in the public domain because its copyright has expired.

31. The 1906 automobile calendar is by Edward Penfield, and is in the collection of the Library of Congress Prints and Photographs Division. It is in the public domain because its copyright has expired.

32. The 50-year perpetual calendar photograph is in the public domain.

33. The 1896 drawing "April" by Eugène Grasset is in the public domain because its copyright has expired.

License Description and Terms

Aside from material purely in the public domain, photographs and other material in this book are used under specific licenses permitting free use, usually with an attribution requirement. For full text and terms of these licenses, click or enter the appropriate links below. If you believe there is an error in the copyright status or attribution of any of these images, please email us.

- Creative Commons Attribution 2.0 Generic (CC-BY 2.0): http://creativecommons.org/licenses/by/2.0/deed.en
- Creative Commons Attribution-Share Alike 3.0 Generic (CC-BY-SA 3.0): http://creativecommons.org/licenses/by-sa/3.0/
- Creative Commons Attribution-Share Alike 2.5 Generic (CC-BY-SA 2.5): http://creativecommons.org/licenses/by-sa/2.5/deed.en
- Creative Commons Attribution-Share Alike 2.0 Generic (CC-BY-SA 2.0): http://creativecommons.org/licenses/by/2.0/deed.en
- Creative Commons Attribution-Share Alike 1.0 Generic (CC-BY-SA 1.0): http://creativecommons.org/licenses/by-sa/1.0/deed.en
- CC0 1.0 Universal (CC0 1.0) Public Domain Dedication (CC0 1.0) http://creativecommons.org/publicdomain/zero/1.0/deed.en
- GNU Free Documentation License (GFDL): http://en.wikipedia.org/wiki/Wikipedia:Text_of_the_GNU_Free_Documentation_License
- License Art Libre (Free Art License): http://artlibre.org

Timespinner
Press

"April," by Eugène Grasset

Other Books from Timespinner Press

The Story of a Special Day
Michael Dobson

A series of (eventually) 366 volumes covering everything that happened on your special day! Events, births, deaths, quotes, holidays, and much more. It's like a birthday card they'll never throw away!

US$7.95 print / US$2.99 ebook.

From Plassey to Pakistan
Humayun Mirza

The history of British Colonial India and the formation of Pakistan from the unique perspective of the son of Pakistan's first president and last of the royal line of Bengal, Bihar, and Orissa! This unique historical document tells the inside story of this distinguished family, including the detailed story of the coup that toppled his father from power!

US$27.95 print

A Whole New Navy: America's War in the Pacific

Miles Durr

The most comprehensive and detailed description of America's naval war in the Pacific ever—every battle, every ship, every task force and every task group from Pearl Harbor through the Japanese surrender! A must-have for the collection of every World War II buff!

US$29.95 print

Improbable History: The Weird, the Obscure, and the Strangely Important

edited by Michael Dobson

From the birth of Western civilization to the rescue of Apollo 13, from the Leaning Tower of Pisa to Florence's Duomo, history has often turned on small, improbable details. Whatever happened to the ancient Samaritan people? Why did a fortuitous rainstorm allow the British to conquer India? How did an air raid in Italy lead to the development of chemotherapy? What happened when Albert Einstein met Adolf Hitler on the streets of Berlin? How did the Japanese manage to attack the US mainland using balloons? A cast of award-winning writers tackle some of the strangest tales in history!

US$19.95 print